Praise for previous edi

"I've recently learned of a new book that addresses questions about the big event ... The author discusses everything from the kinds of questions to ask the bride and her mother beforehand to how to welcome guests and handle toasts."

VIRGINIA LEEMING
The Vancouver Sun

"As a wedding master of ceremonies, Tom Haibeck made all the mistakes ... Haibeck, a Vancouver marketing consultant, knows preparation is the key."

STEPHEN BARRINGTON
Canadian Press

"It's a terrific little book. It tells you everything you need to know."

INGRID TAMMEN
LG-73 Radio

"Most people have no idea how difficult it can be to emcee some sort of event. This is a handy little book for them."

BILL GOOD
CKNW Radio

"Local PR man Tom Haibeck has been there. After emceeing a lot of weddings and suffering through some bad emcees at others, he has prepared a guide to help you through someone else's big day."

TOM WALTERS
UTV

"I've emceed hundreds of events and I still find The Wedding MC book to be a valuable source of education and inspiration."

SCOTT BARRATT
JR Country Radio

"The wedding emcee guide is an invaluable handbook."

STEVIE MITCHELL
The Courier

I found your book extremely helpful! True to the Boy Scout motto, I learned to 'Be Prepared' - and it worked!"

MARK MCPHERSON
Miami, Florida

"Thank heaven for The Wedding MC. I — who hate standing up before a crowd — was emcee at my nephew's wedding recently, and your book not only made it all bearable, but it also made me look good."

PAUL GRESCOE
Vancouver, British Columbia

"It covers everything they need to know, from how to help plan and preside over the evening to how to write and propose a compelling toast. As a matter of fact, I sent both my sons a copy when they were married and the book helped ensure that each of their weddings was a great success."

LINDA REDMOND
Associate Publisher, Wedding Bells Magazine

THE
WEDDING
MC

A Complete Guide to Success
for the Best Man or Event Host

Written by Tom Haibeck
Illustrations by Grahame Arnould

First printing in April, 1990
Reprinted in October, 1993
Reprinted in December, 1998
Reprinted in April, 2000
Reprinted in November, 2002
Reprinted in May, 2004
Reprinted in March, 2005
U.S. edition: Printed in March, 2005

Library of Congress Control Number: 2005922668

ISBN: 0-9697051-2-3

1. Wedding etiquette.   2. Weddings — Planning.
3. Masters of ceremonies. I. Title.
BJ2065.M37H34 1993   395'.22   C93-091307-8

Printed in the United States of America
by United Graphics, Incorporated

Published by:
The Haibeck Communications Group Inc.
Suite 502, 3608 Deercrest Drive
North Vancouver, British Columbia, Canada V7G 2S8

Telephone: (604) 924-5351
Fax: (604) 924-5358
Web: WeddingToasts.com
E-Mail: tom@haibeck.com

The Haibeck Group
STRATEGIC MARKETING & COMMUNICATIONS

This book is dedicated to the joy of a wedding – and to all the people who contribute to that special day.

It is also an exercise in personal philanthropy – as 15% of my royalties from this book will be donated to Mothers Against Drunk Driving.

Wedding receptions are indeed a celebration. As such, they often involve a lot of alcohol. Given the nature of the celebration, guests sometimes drink more than they normally would. And far too often, those guests then try to drive home while impaired, thereby jeopardizing the lives of others.

Families hosting a wedding need to take an active role in encouraging their guests not to drink and drive (and that message should be part of the script for every wedding emcee). In fact, if your wedding features an open bar, you (as host) could face massive liabilities should one of your guests drink, drive and be involved in a serious car accident.

Mothers Against Drunk Driving is a non-profit, grassroots organization that is committed to stopping impaired driving and supporting the victims of this violent crime.

It is a volunteer-driven organization that includes not only mothers, but fathers, friends, business professionals, experts in the impaired driving field and concerned citizens who want to make a difference in the fight against impaired driving.

For more information, please visit www.MADD.org or call the organization's toll-free phone line at 1-800-GET-MADD (438-6233).

Contents

Foreword

Weddings are my business. Over the past twelve years, I have helped plan and have provided entertainment services for over 600 wedding receptions in Southern California and across America.

During that time, I have seen my share of wedding reception disasters. From drunken speeches and inappropriate toasts to out-of-control guests who have turned an otherwise beautiful wedding into a free-for-all, I know firsthand just how devastating those kinds of experiences can be for the bride and groom and for their families.

That's why I am happy to recommend The Wedding MC handbook. The concept of having a designated emcee to preside over the wedding reception is an excellent way to make sure the event stays on track, the couple's wishes are met and the guests have a memorable and enjoyable time.

This little book contains everything you need to know about serving as a wedding emcee in a humorous, easy-to-read fashion. I consider it "must read" material for anyone asked to help plan, speak at or emcee a wedding reception

Peter Merry, President
American Disc Jockey Association

An Introduction To This Book

According to "Bride" magazine, the average American wedding costs $18,874. Guess which part of the wedding costs the most?

The answer is the wedding reception. It's an event that typically consumes nearly half of the overall wedding budget, ringing in at $7,246 to feed an average of 186 guests.

That's a lot of money for most families. And sadly, far too many of those high-priced wedding receptions never meet the family's expectations. Instead of the joyous gala envisioned by the happy couple, they wind up being dull, anxiety-ridden events characterized by long-winded speeches, ill-advised attempts at humor and a general lack of direction and purpose.

Worse, some wedding receptions devolve into absolute horror shows that are long remembered for all the wrong reasons.

It's ironic that while the wedding couple may spend endless hours agonizing over guest lists and wedding vows and bridesmaids' dresses and stationery and photo opportunities and flower arrangements and bridal registries and countless other details, they too often ignore or leave to chance the key element that can often make or break their Big Day. And that is the reception itself.

A wedding reception is an event – and as such, it demands a high degree of planning and a great deal of thought. Yet many couples assume that the evening's events will just fall into place, or that the best man or the disc jockey or the band leader will take charge of the event and make sure everything goes smoothly.

But when the reception gets underway and the happy couple suddenly realizes they hadn't given any thought to how to get the 186 guests seated, they both begin to get a little anxious. No problem, the best man can make an announcement. But the best man is nowhere to be found – he's rehearsing his speech in the men's room (the one he penned on the back of a napkin on the flight from Boston).

Panicked, the bride's mother tries to wave people into the dining room. But no one can hear her, as the open bar has made for a raucous crowd.

The bride's frazzled father storms to the podium to grab the microphone. He flicks the switich to turn on the mike, but there's no power because the audio-visual technician turned off the sound before heading outside for a smoke.

Finally, the catering manager is located in the bowels of the kitchen. He's working under incredible pressure, trying to juggle the wedding in the main ballroom, a bar mitzvah on the patio and a corporate event upstairs. But after some discussion (during which he loudly admonishes the bride's mother for leaving everything to the last minute), he reluctantly agrees to marshal his team of servers into the reception area to help move people into the dining room.

The guests are now seated, and the noise in the room grows louder as they introduce themselves and get re-acquainted with old friends and distant relatives. Meanwhile, the wedding party is assembled outside the dining room, ready to make its grand entrance. But wait – shouldn't someone announce their entry? Again, it's too loud for anyone to shout over the crowd and the microphone is still dead. So they march in unannounced, and make their way to the head table before the audience fully realizes their entrance. A smattering of applause starts and then fizzles.

With the entire room now seated, the minister goes to the podium to offer a blessing before dinner. But the groom's 83-year-old grandfather, who has said the blessing at every other family event during the past 45 years, is miffed because he had prepared a special blessing for his favorite grandson and his new bride.

The minister smiles at the crowd, leans forward and begins to utter the words to his earnest prayer. But the AV guy has just returned from his break and hasn't yet been able to set the proper levels on the sound system. Feedback from the amplifiers squeal through the microphone, upstaging the minister's blessing and nearly blowing the eardrums of guests sitting closest to the speakers.

As the minister returns to his seat, there's a pregnant pause in the proceedings, and no one seems to know what to do. Dinner is still to be served, and the bride and groom look at each other as if to ask *"What's next?"* Sensing the moment, Uncle Buck staggers to the podium. He's personally taste-tested every brand of whiskey at the open bar, and with double-scotch in hand, he offers his heartfelt congratulations to his beautiful niece and her new husband (whose name escapes him).

But it gets worse. The best man, not to be outdone, delivers a 47-minute speech to recount "life back at the frat house." The bride is close to tears, as the best man decides to close his speech with a vivid account of the groom's adventures at his bachelor dinner. The boys in the back of the room are howling with laughter; the bride's mother's blood-pressure has now reached an all-time high; the catering manager is livid because 186 dinners have gone cold waiting for the best man to finish his speech; and the guests begin to buzz about how such a beautiful wedding could turn into such a comedic disaster.

Scenes like that unfold every weekend in hotels and meeting facilities around the world. An event that represents one of the biggest days – and one of the biggest expenditures – in the life of a family is needlessly marred or even ruined by a combination of poor planning, miscommunication, inappropriate speeches, plus an overall lack of understanding about what it takes to make a successful event happen.

My own experience with such an event prompted me to write this book. Despite the fact that I was employed in the public relations industry and had managed some of our city's biggest corporate events, our wedding had traces of the disaster described above. Again, we assumed things would happen as they should – but they didn't.

That experience – together with the fact that I have been asked to plan, emcee and/or speak at dozens of different weddings, corporate and community events – convinced me that there was a need for this kind of step-by-step handbook. And I was right – it has become a perennial best-seller, with over 50,000 sold to date.

The book contains everything you need to know about how to make the most of a wedding reception. While I wrote it for the specific purposes of the emcee and/or the best man, it will prove helpful to the bride and groom, their parents or anyone else asked to help plan or speak at a wedding reception.

In many parts of the world, it is customary for the best man to also serve as the emcee for the wedding reception. That's not always the case – for if the best man has a bad case of stage fright and isn't comfortable in the role of emcee, an alternative is for another close friend or relative to serve as the wedding emcee. Another option is to hire a professional disc jockey to serve as the emcee for both the reception dinner and the dance.

No matter who takes on that role, I am absolutely convinced of the need for it. Again, a wedding reception is an event – and as any event planner will tell you, an event needs a Master of Ceremonies. Someone has to step forward and take charge of that event. They need to work with the couple (and perhaps their parents) well in advance of the event to determine an agenda which clearly identifies how the event is to unfold, the timing for each segment of it, who is to speak or offer a toast, when that is to happen, how they are to be introduced plus all the other subtle details that are so often overlooked.

In fairness, planning a wedding reception is an entirely new experience for most couples. They simply don't have the knowledge and experience to know what needs to be done, nor the time to properly research and put together a great event.

But aside from the mechanics of the event, a good emcee can add needed warmth and personality to a wedding reception. They can help ensure it lives up to its expectations, whether that be a classy, formal affair or more relaxed and informal occasion. They can also help ensure that those embarrassing 47-minute frat house rambles never occur, and that toasts and wedding speeches meet the expected guidelines for good taste.

In the short time it takes to read this book, the best man and/or wedding emcee will develop a much fuller understanding of what it takes to preside over what should be a fun, engaging and truly memorable event. And because it demands plenty of interaction with those responsible for the event (the new couple and/or their parents), it will provide a fail-safe way to ensure their vision of that special day is honored and acted upon.

For some people, all of those details will be expertly handled by a professional wedding planner, who will in turn enlist the services of a professional disc jockey. That's a great option – if you can afford it. But the fact is, most people can't.

Let's be clear: A professional DJ can do wonders for a wedding reception dance (following the dinner). That's what they're good at – and they can put together an excellent show with very little advance preparation. But if you expect them to take on dual roles as both MC for the reception dinner *and* as DJ for the dance that follows, you might be disappointed.

Most professional disc jockeys simply won't devote the time or go to the trouble to properly prepare for an additional role as wedding emcee – unless you pay them a much higher fee. After all, time is money in their business. Don't expect them to invest the extra hours it will take to do what's required unless you are prepared to properly pay them for those additional services.

Again, if you can afford to do so, great (most DJs will do an excellent job as MC if properly paid). If not, I strongly recommend you enlist the best man, a close friend or a relative to work with you in doing what is outlined in this book. Trust me: Based on my experience – and that of the 50,000+ who have bought this book – a close friend or relative can do a first-class job in emceeing a wedding.

The other key advantage that a close friend or relative has over the professional DJ (in acting as MC) is the fact that he or she is truly connected with the couple. A favorite uncle of the bride or a close friend of the groom can bring a unique blend of knowledge and personalized experience to the wedding reception that simply can't be duplicated by a professional.

They are authentic – they share a very real connection with the couple, their families and their friends. And that connection will usually translate into a much warmer, more moving and far more intimate wedding reception dinner than one that is hosted by a paid professional.

Ask yourself: Would you hire a DJ to host your family's Thanksgiving dinner? Probably not. So in keeping with that line of thought, why hire a professional to host your family's wedding reception?

A close friend or family member is also uniquely motivated to succeed in the role of wedding emcee. Why? Because they have an ongoing relationship with those in attendance. And believe me, no one wants to fail miserably in front of a group of people that they will continue to see at family dinners and events for many years to come. This isn't just another gig for them – it's an honor and a privilege to help some very special people in their lives commemorate one of the biggest days in their lives.

It's also an opportunity for them to shine. While the spotlight should indeed be on the bride and groom, the wedding emcee will be front and centre at the podium. That has a way of galvanizing the attention of that particular individual – and often inspires him or her to devote an inordinate amount of time and effort in preparing for their role. That usually translates into a superb performance at the wedding itself.

To summarize: If you have the budget and are more comfortable going with a professional, do so. But if budget is an issue and/or you would prefer to add a more genuine, familial element to your wedding, ask the best man, a friend or family member to serve as emcee. Trust me – that person can do an excellent job, given the opportunity. Just give them a copy of this book, and work with them on the steps that follow. If you *are* the emcee, let's get started!

This seventh edition of the Wedding MC handbook has been expanded yet again to include more material on how to prepare for The Big Day. From toasting tips and ideas on how to write a truly outstanding wedding speech to the nuts and bolts of constructing a proper agenda for the wedding reception, you will find a wealth of information in this book that has been gleaned from my 25+ years of experience with weddings, speeches and special events.

It also contains a selection of cleverly-penned cartoons by cartoonist Grahame Arnould to illustrate how NOT to go about emceeing a wedding (our inspiration for the character drawn was "Uncle Buck," the loud and rather loutish uncle of our fictional bride). Thank you, Grahame, for some truly hilarious material.

Thanks also to Chuck Davis for his eagle-eyed editing; Peter Merry for writing the Foreword section; Hank Leonhardt for his brilliant cover design; Brian Ritchie of Detour Creative for his meticulous typesetting and pre-press mastery; the gang at Kent Kallberg Photography for all the re-touching they had to do to my portrait; the computing science team at the British Columbia Institute of Technology for their outstanding work on WeddingToasts.com; the good people at Greenleaf Book Group for their assistance in helping me to expand distribution into the United States; and the many thoughtful individuals who have taken the time to offer their comments, suggestions and tributes.

I sincerely hope this book helps you make the most of your role as best man and/or wedding emcee. Please let me know how it goes – write me an e-mail (see address below) and tell me about your experience (include a picture if you can). I would also welcome any ideas you would like to share with others through future editions of this book. And of course, testimonials are always appreciated.

Cheers – and here's to your success!

> Tom Haibeck
> tom@haibeck.com
> Phone: (604) 924-5351
> Fax: (604) 924-5358
> Web: WeddingToasts.com

"Food fight!"

"And Now....
Heeere's Johnny!"

*An old friend or relative has just called and asked
if you would mind acting as Best Man & Master
of Ceremonies at an upcoming wedding. You've
agreed and now you're starting to panic ...*

I've never done this before, you suddenly realize. What exactly
does a "best man" do? For that matter, what does a "wedding
emcee" do? Will I have to make a speech? What if I bomb in
front of my friends and family? What if nobody laughs when I
crack a joke? What should I say when I make a toast? How will
I remember all my lines, let alone everyone's name? What if the
microphone doesn't work? Microphone? My God, I've never
even used a microphone! Why did I ever agree to do this in the
first place???

This book has been written to help you through that period of
anxiety leading up to the wedding and to help prepare you to
do a first-class job as the Master of Ceremonies and/or the Best
Man at the wedding itself.

Having served as emcee at many weddings, dinners and special
events, I've developed a pretty good understanding of what
works and what doesn't. I've been in your shoes many times
and experienced the gut-wrenching anxiety many of you may be
feeling about now.

I have also enjoyed the honor of being best man at a variety of weddings, so I know what you can expect in that role as well. And finally, I've taken that long trip down the aisle myself, and have vivid memories of how the bride and groom are feeling about now – and what they expect of you.

Reading this book won't turn you into a clone of David Letterman or Jay Leno. Nor will it pave the way for you to become a professional emcee or comedian. But it will offer some good, honest, down-to-earth advice on helping the bride and groom make the most of their special day, ensuring that the guests enjoy themselves, and making sure you look good at the same time.

If you'll take the time to read this book and follow through on the recommended steps and procedures outlined in it, you will be fully prepared to do an outstanding job as Master of Ceremonies at the upcoming wedding. What might feel like an incredible burden to you right now may well turn into one of the greatest nights of your life, for there are few greater joys than to earn the laughter and applause of an appreciative audience of wedding guests.

But more importantly, you will play a pivotal role in the success of the wedding -- as through your efforts, the union of those two souls will be celebrated in style at an event that will long be remembered for all the right reasons.

Think of it this way: the bride and groom have entrusted you with a very important responsibility and will expect that you take your job seriously. In helping you through that task, I'm going to ask that you go above and beyond what most people would do. And believe me, it will be worth the effort.

Being asked to emcee a wedding is a great honor. It takes some work, but usually results in a lot of fun, both for you and everyone else involved. Bear that in mind as you read this book and prepare yourself for The Big Day – after all, having fun is what it's all about.

So let's get to lesson one: The Duties of a Wedding MC (we'll talk about the Best Man's duties a little later).

The Duties of a Wedding MC

Simply stated, your job is to preside over the wedding reception. Just as a meeting needs a chairman, so, too, does a wedding reception need a host or MC. Someone has to be responsible for making sure the show gets on the road and stays on the road.

The bride and groom have probably chosen you for the job because you have a talent for keeping things under control and a certain amount of confidence in assuming that role. The couple no doubt has enough on their minds without having to worry about the reception itself and so they have asked you to take charge. And that's exactly what you should do – take charge!

Now please don't confuse this with taking charge of the wedding itself. The bride and her mother will have plenty to say about that and will have spent many hours planning and coordinating the day.

Depending upon what format the reception takes, you may be required to direct guests to dinner, introduce the head table, read messages from those unable to attend, achnowledge special guests, deliver a toast, smooth over a few rough spots, introduce other speakers and coordinate the traditional cake-cutting ceremony.

You may also be asked to help plan the reception program, and so be prepared to offer suggestions and guidance if necessary. The next chapter offers a sample agenda and some notes to follow in planning the wedding reception. But please remember at all times to be sensitive towards the wishes of the wedding couple and their parents – it is, after all, their special day.

*"So before we discuss what you want,
let's discuss my vision for the reception."*

Planning the Reception

Like any party, wedding receptions take many forms. Some are staged in elaborate ballrooms. Others unfold in someone's backyard. Dinner may be served for several hundred guests. Or a few close friends might gather around a bottle of champagne.

Whatever format the reception takes will be determined by the overall budget for the wedding, the number of people invited, where it is held, and the personal preferences of the wedding couple and their families.

That format, however, is of critical importance to the Master of Ceremonies. After all, your job is to help ensure that the reception is carried out in the manner intended by the couple and their families. And if you are to be successful in that role, you must have a full understanding of what is expected of you within the format of the reception itself.

Therefore, I strongly recommend that you set up a meeting with the key decision-makers involved in the reception several weeks (or even better, several months) prior to the wedding. In most cases, that will be the bride and her mother; bear in mind, however, that the groom and his parents may also have some ideas to contribute to that process.

Get together in a quiet place where you won't be interrupted and plan to take at least an hour to complete your discussions. Bring a pencil and this book, which contains a worksheet for you to fill in with important information that you must know (see "Questions to Ask the Bride & Her Mother" and "The Evening's Agenda").

Your primary objective in holding this meeting is to work out a written agenda for the reception itself and to gain as much information as possible about where it will be held, the number of guests expected, the general format for the wedding, special family traditions, etc.

The agenda should identify who is involved and list the order of events, with a time-frame for their completion. It should be put in writing and distributed: to the bride and her parents, for their approval; the groom and his parents; any other key decision-makers involved in the reception; people who will be making toasts; those responsible for the preparation and serving of refreshments; and entertainers booked to perform. Make sure everyone knows what's happening before it all starts happening.

As much as possible, try to create agreement at the meeting(s) about how the event is to unfold. That can prevent a lot of needless angst and embarrassment at the wedding itself.

Case in point: I once witnessed two very high profile politicians nearly come to blows over who was to cut the official ribbon at the opening of a major public facility. It was ugly and, in fact, ridiculous. But it was all conducted behind closed doors, well in advance of the event. They eventually agreed to cut the ribbon in a manner that permitted both of them to participate in the process.

Here is a sample agenda for your reference in planning a "sit-down" reception. Some thoughts on each part of this agenda follow later. Please remember, though, that this is simply a suggested agenda; there is no universally recognized "etiquette" to govern a wedding reception, so do what works best for the bridal couple, their families and you.

AGENDA FOR HUDSON/O'FLYNN WEDDING

The Fairmont Plaza Hotel – June 18, 2005

6:55 Guests to be seated before bridal party is seated. MC to ask guests to rise when the bridal party makes its entrance and is seated.

7:00 MC to welcome guests on behalf of new couple, introduce self, make toast to the new couple, ask Minister Reeves to say grace.

7:05 MC to invite guests to help themselves to buffet dinner, starting with tables to his immediate left.

7:15 MC to remind guests of alternatives to clinking spoons on glasses to encourage Bride and Groom to kiss each other.

7:40 While dessert is being served, MC to read messages from guests unable to attend, introduce guests who traveled long distances.

7:45 MC to introduce head table, then call upon Ed Bergen, friend of the Hudson family, to give Toast to the Bride.

7:55 MC to introduce Groom – Ryan O'Flynn, who responds to toast, thanks Bride's parents, offers Toast to the Bridesmaids.

8:00 MC to introduce Best Man – Dave Johnson, who offers a speech about the Groom and a Toast to the Mothers of the Bride and Groom.

8:05 MC to introduce Father of Bride – Fred Hudson, who thanks guests for attending the wedding.

8:10 MC relates a few more humorous stories about Bride and Groom, calls upon couple to cut cake.

8:25 After cake is cut, MC to introduce entertainment, encourage guests to dance and enjoy themselves.

11:00 MC to invite single women to gather in centre of dance floor for bouquet toss by Bride; to be followed by Groom's garter toss to bachelors.

"Kiss, smooch, squeeze, grab her by the ..."

Preparing the Agenda

The sample agenda on the previous page lists the approximate times for specific events, the order in which they will happen, and who is responsible for doing what.

It's the same kind of agenda that I would put together if I were planning a major event or reception for one of my public relations clients. It provides structure for the event and ties together all the various elements that will go into it. For just as a movie needs a script, an event needs an agenda.

An event agenda also provides a way to create written agreement amongst the various parties as to what will happen at the reception, the order in which things will happen, approximate times for completion of each key segment of the event and confirmation as to who is to be responsible for the various elements of the program (e.g., "Uncle Charlie to make the Toast to the Bride at 8:30 PM").

Of all the recommendations made in this book, this step ranks amongst the most important, in my opinion. As mentioned, these kinds of details need to be thoroughly discussed and resolved well in advance of the wedding reception, when everyone's mind is clear and their attention is focused.

Advance planning also enables you to bring together the myriad of parties that may be involved in the reception, from the families themselves to the various professionals involved (caterers, disc jockey, band, etc.). Trying to chase down everyone the day before the event will be difficult, at best. And having been through a bad case of pre-wedding jitters, I can tell you that the wedding party will have enough on its collective mind in the days leading up to the wedding without having to worry about the timing for Uncle Charlie's toast.

If you can all meet face-to-face, do so. But if you live in a different city than the bride and groom (and others involved in the event), hold your planning sessions over the phone, and follow-up with everyone via e-mail. And if you are reading this book and starting to feel like the other people involved should be made more aware of the importance of this process, you might suggest they purchase an eBook version of The Wedding MC handbook on-line from my website at *WeddingToasts.com* (it's the exact same book, and can be instantly downloaded from the website for just $9.95 US). It will make an enormous difference having everyone on the same page, so to speak.

As mentioned, the sample agenda is simply a suggested sequence of events; the bride and her mother may want you to do certain things in another order, and you may be more comfortable adding or deleting certain elements from your program. Whatever you decide to do, make sure it is written down, that it receives proper approval, and that other key people involved in the reception program know what's going on.

Timing is particularly important. You must know when the refreshments will be served so that guests' glasses are filled when it's time to make toasts. You must also know what time the program should start and end, when the entertainers are scheduled to perform, what time the bride and groom would like to leave and when guests should leave if the hall must be cleared by a certain time (all of these points are included in the section on "Questions to Ask the Bride & Her Mother").

If possible, I would encourage you to keep the reception program itself (that is, the speeches and toasts that follow the dinner or refreshments) to a maximum of a half hour. Unless all speakers are particularly eloquent or entertaining, to go beyond twenty or thirty minutes will probably strain the audience's attention. Suggest that individuals offering toasts keep their speeches to five minutes or less (but be tactful in doing this).

Keep your watch before you at all times during the reception, along with your agenda. If the program starts to drag or goes off-course for some reason, try to cut down on your own material. Similarly, be prepared to offer some "fill" if the program goes too fast (a couple of jokes or stories, one-liners or anecdotes about the bride and groom).

Be flexible. Unexpected changes can often alter the course of events for even the best-planned weddings, and it's your job to try to smooth things over when they happen (remember that the "bloopers" or "out-takes" section of most DVDs contain some of the funniest and most spontaneous humor to be found in the entire production. So if possible, try to laugh along with things if they start to go awry). Relax and remain confident at all times – after all, you're in charge.

Let's re-visit the reception agenda now with some thoughts on putting it all together.

THE BRIDE & GROOM'S ENTRANCE

Your first duty may be to ask the wedding guests to stand and welcome members of the bridal party as they make their entrance into the reception area. At some weddings, the guests are expected to applaud the bridal party's entrance (if that's the case, be sure to start the applause). Ask the guests to be seated once the bridal party has been seated.

WELCOME TO GUESTS

A good way to start the program is to welcome guests on behalf of the wedding couple and to then introduce yourself. *"On behalf of the new Mr. and Mrs. _____, I welcome you to this joyous occasion. My name is _____, and I'm ...."* (give your relationship to the wedding party — friend, relative, or whatever). If it is a stand-up reception, call upon the guests to gather around the wedding couple before starting.

THE TOAST TO THE NEW COUPLE

You may want to offer a toast to the new couple at this point, but keep it short and sweet. *"Ladies and gentlemen, please join me in toasting the new Mr. and Mrs. _____."*

THE BLESSING

Ask the person who is to say grace to proceed. *"I'd now like to call upon _____ to say grace."*

THE DINNER

If the dinner is being served by the catering staff, there is probably no need to make any further announcements until dessert comes. If the dinner is buffet style, you may want to announce which tables are to help themselves first:*"Ladies and gentlemen, please help yourselves to the buffet, starting with the tables to my immediate right."* In some cases, the catering staff may want to say something about the dinner as well, so check with them beforehand. You may also want to acknowledge the caterers after dinner with a round of applause. Your goal is to generate as much postive energy as possible in that room!

THE CLINKING OF SPOONS ON GLASSES

Ask the bride and groom if they would like you to make an announcement about this practice, which signals them to kiss one another. Sometimes it can get tiresome, and the wedding couple may want you to ask the guests to do something else.

For example, you might invite guests (or the table at which they are sitting) to come forward during the dinner and sing a song with the word "love" in it (rather than clink glasses). This can be a lot of fun, as it encourages the guests (individually or in a group) to let their hair down and get into the act. It will also help break the ice for the toasts and for your presentation.

Another option: Ask couples in the audience to kiss, with the proviso that the bride and groom must kiss each other in the same manner. Believe me, this can lead to some side-splitting displays of affection when people pucker up and ham it up.

JOKES/ANNOUNCEMENTS DURING DINNER

You might tell a few humorous stories during dinner to keep the evening moving. In my experience, however, it's usually best to let the guests enjoy their dinner and chat amongst themselves before you start your presentation.

MESSAGES/SPECIAL GUESTS

I like to take care of this part of the program while dessert is being served. The messages can make for some fairly easy material to get a laugh (especially if you make up a couple of humorous ones -- suggestion: *"Congratulations Sheila on your big day. We'll miss you. Signed, Bob .... Ed ... Tony ... Mike ... Rupert ... and Big Al."*)

The practice of acknowledging special guests (elderly relatives, people who have traveled a long way to attend the wedding) also helps to focus the audience's attention on themselves rather than on you. This can help relieve some of the pressure you may be feeling in starting the program. It's also an excellent means of winning the audience's support and attention.

RE-INTRODUCE YOURSELF

When you introduced yourself at the very start of the program, you didn't go into much detail other than to state your relationship to the wedding couple (e.g. *"I'm Mary's Uncle"*). You might want to re-introduce yourself at this point with a phrase such as *"in case you've forgotten who I am"* or *"you're probably wondering all about me."*

I would recommend doing this because: a) audiences like to know something about the person they're listening to, and b) if you plan to make any humorous but disparaging remarks about someone else in the wedding party, they'll probably go over better if you've poked a bit of fun at yourself first. If you do re-introduce yourself at this point, though, keep it light and brief. And if you don't feel comfortable doing this, don't.

INTRODUCE THE HEAD TABLE

Wedding guests always enjoy knowing a bit of background on each member of the wedding party – and the wedding party will feel honored to be acknowledged with a brief introduction. Start at one end of the table and introduce each of the bridesmaids and groomsmen before re-introducing the wedding couple. If you have done your homework, you will have chatted with each member of the wedding party before the wedding to learn where they are from, what they do for a living, how they met the wedding couple – that kind of thing. This information can make for some excellent comedy material by embellishing it a bit or by pointing out some of the quirks or eccentricities of each individual.

TOAST TO THE BRIDE

Now that your audience has been introduced to the head table guests, it's time to call upon people to make a few toasts. The first toast is always to the bride and/or new couple and is often made by the best man, a close friend or a relative (this person may or may not be sitting at the head table). Make sure everyone's glass is filled before calling upon the person who is to make this toast.

THE GROOM'S RESPONSE

It's customary for the groom to respond to the toast made to his new bride by offering his own toast to any or all of the following: the bridesmaids, the mother of the bride, parents of the bride, his own parents; other special people. While introducing the groom, though, you might want to tell a few humorous stories about him and perhaps his new wife. Or, you can leave this until after the groom has made his toast(s).

OTHER TOASTS

If there are other toasts to be made, make sure you know about them in advance, and that they are on the agenda. When introducing people who are about to make a toast, keep the introduction short and sweet: *"I'd now like to call upon Mr. Bert Ostlund, who is a friend of the groom, to offer a toast to the bridesmaids."*

In my experience, it's a good idea for the emcee to introduce each person making a toast. What often happens is that once the first toast is made, the audience continues to buzz and a second toast can easily be drowned out (especially if the person making the toast doesn't have a strong presence or speaking voice). Intros also provide a nice "bridge" between toasts.

FATHER OF THE BRIDE THANKS GUESTS

The bride's father might want to thank all guests at this point for attending the wedding; he may also want to say a couple of nice things about his new son-in-law (this is strictly optional, of course).

THE CAKE-CUTTING CEREMONY

The toasts and formal part of the program are usually followed by the traditional cake-cutting ceremony. Invite the couple to cut the cake, and those with cameras to come forward to take pictures. Make sure the event photographer(s) are fully prepared for the historic moment when knife meets icing.

ANNOUNCE THE EVENING'S ENTERTAINMENT

If a band, disc jockey or other entertainers have been booked to perform, introduce them and let them take over from there. A good way to make the transition is for the band or disc jockey to then introduce the couple's selected music for their first dance.

THE BOUQUET TOSS

Later in the evening, you may announce the bouquet toss by inviting the single women to gather in the middle of the dance floor to try to catch the bouquet thrown by the bride. You may also invite all bachelors to catch the bride's garter, as thrown by the groom. Confirmed bachelors might also be invited to stay clear of the toss.

THE SEND-OFF

After the bride and groom have returned to the reception in their going-away clothes, you may want to announce their "send-off" by asking the guests to gather around them, wish them good luck and send them on their way by throwing rice and confetti. On the other hand, the bride and groom may wish to quietly slip away without having a big fuss made out of their departure – discuss this with them prior to the reception.

"I got it, I got it...!"

Questions to Ask the Bride & Her Mother

Now that you have learned the importance of advance planning and the need to nail down an agenda, here are some questions to review with the decision-makers (who are usually the bride and her mother).

Try to go through these at least a month before the wedding (if possible) to give everyone time to do what's required. The answers to these questions will ultimately help determine how the reception will unfold and what it is expected of you – so take your time, give them some careful thought and make sure everyone is clear on what gets decided.

I would strongly recommend that you follow-up this meeting with a written summary of your understanding of what was decided (just some point form notes about key things). You should also prepare a detailed copy of the actual agenda (see sample).

If you're not great at taking notes or writing summaries, ask someone else in the group to do so. I can't stress enough the importance of having a written record of what gets decided and what the actual agenda will look like. Believe me, things get lost in translation, people forget what was agreed upon and confusion too often reigns in the days leading up to the wedding. So get it down on paper and make sure all of the decision-makers are in agreement.

As mentioned, if possible, try to meet with the decision-makers in person. That will enable everyone to participate in the discussion at the same time, hasten decision-making and help ensure that everyone's input is properly considered. Ideally, the discussion should take place at the actual reception venue, with the caterer and other key suppliers in attendance.

If you and the decision-makers live in different cities and it's impossible to meet in person prior to the week of the wedding, try to coordinate a tele-conference to bring everyone together. E-mail or instant messaging can also be helpful as a means to follow-up. Make sure you exchange contact information with everyone at this meeting.

In reviewing the questions that follow, you can either write down the corresponding number to each question on a piece of paper and then fill in the answers as you go; OR, you can go to my website at www.WeddingToasts.com and download the sample template pages that list these questions.

Another template at that site offers a worksheet for you to use in filling out an agenda for the evening's events.

A final word on this meeting: Weddings, like any special event, can be fraught with politics. Different people may have different ideas of how the reception should be structured and what needs to be done.

My advice to you, as the Master of Ceremonies at that wedding, is to try to avoid getting caught up in the decision-making. This isn't your event – it's simply yours to preside over. The bride and her mother and other family members will make those decisions; your role at the planning session(s) is to simply try to lead the decision-makers through the process by posing the following questions.

Once these questions are addressed, you then need to confirm (by way of writing) what was decided and ensure that you understand what is expected of you as Master of Ceremonies. With all of that confirmed, you will be ready to roll.

Questions to Ask the Bride & Her Mother:

1. Where will the reception be held?

2. What is the actual address of the reception venue? Phone number? Fax number? E-mail address? Contact person?

3. Does the facility have a website (to preview)?

4. Is it difficult to find – will you need directions on how to get there?

5. What time are you expected to be at the reception?

6. Can you gain access to the reception venue well in advance of the wedding day (to preview, rehearse and get a sense of how the event will flow)?

7. Who will be the contact person for the MC during the wedding reception (the bride or her mother or someone else)?

8. How many guests are expected?

9. Is it a stand-up reception or a sit-down dinner?

10. If it is a sit-down dinner, will it be buffet style or will guests be served their meals?

11. What time will dinner and/or refreshments be served?

12. Who will be responsible for asking guests to be seated?

13. Should serving staff (or others) be asked to help move the guests from the reception area into the dining area?

14. Will the bridal party make a special entrance that needs to be announced?

15. If so, who will cue the MC that the bridal party is ready to make their entrance?

16. Once the head table is seated, should the MC offer a toast to the new couple or introduce members of the wedding party?

17. Is there to be a blessing before dinner? If so, who will offer the blessing?

18. Are there any special announcements to be made about the dinner or the refreshments? (For example, do guests need to be directed to the buffet or to the open bar, etc.)

19. What does the couple want said about the traditional clinking of glasses during dinner to prompt them to kiss each other?

20. Will there be a public address system?

21. Will there be an audio technician or disc jockey at the reception to operate the sound system?

22. When would be a good time to do a pre-reception sound check?

23. Will there be a podium?

24. Will the MC speak from a stage or at the head table?

25. Where will the MC sit through dinner?

26. Where will the toasts/speeches be delivered from?

27. Does anyone require a hand-held microphone? Other audio-visual tools (for example, a laptop and projector for a PowerPoint presentation to accompany a toast)?

28. Does anyone who will be making a toast need some extra help with their toast or a briefing on the use of a microphone?

29. At what point should the main program begin?

30. Who will toast the new bride/new couple?

31. Does the groom (and/or the bride) want to respond to that toast?

32. Who will toast the bridesmaids?

33. Are there any other toasts to be made?

34. Does the father of the bride want to say anything?

35. Does the father of the groom want to say anything?

36. Does anyone else want to say anything?

37. Are there any special family traditions to be upheld?

38. Are there any special guests to be acknowledged?

39. Will there be any special e-mails to be read from well-wishers unable to attend?

40. If so, who will provide them to the MC?

41. What are the names of the head-table guests?

42. Would it be appropriate to offer some background information on each person in introducing them?

43. If so, would it be appropriate to contact each individual and conduct a brief interview prior to the wedding? Contact info?

44. Is anyone's name difficult to pronounce?

45. How would you describe the audience? Elderly and conservative? Religious? Young and hip? A mixture?

46. Do we need to be especially aware of offending anyone with humorous stories or one-liners that they might consider offensive?

47. Is there to be a disc jockey, band or other performers?

48. If so, how is the transition to be made from MC to DJ/band?

49. Who is to announce the cake-cutting?

50. Who will announce the first dance?

51. Will there be a bouquet toss – and if so, when?

52. Will there be a garter scramble – and if so, when?

53. At what time do the bride and groom want to leave?

54. How will the bride and groom be sent off?

55. Are there any other announcements that need to be made?

56. By what time must all guests leave?

57. Does the host want to offer safe transportation home for any guest that has been drinking?

58. Is there anything else we need to review?

59. Who needs to be copied on the agenda and meeting summary that will follow?

"And isn't that a beautiful bride's dress? Must have cost a fortune — all that extra material."

Preparing Your Presentation

Now that you have met with the bride and her mother, prepared an agenda and gotten approval from the powers-that-be to proceed with that agenda, it's time to begin preparing a few speaking notes for the occasion.

Look at each part of the agenda, and start to think about what you will say at each point. Try to give yourself plenty of time to get inspired about this – preferably several weeks to let your thoughts come together. As those thoughts come to mind, be sure to write them down. They may drift away if you don't record them. I like to carry a specific notebook for this purpose; another option is to set up a file to store your notes.

After you've spent a few weeks thinking about your presentation, you'll probably have several pages of notes to sift through and organize. I suggest you avoid the temptation to write out your presentation word-for-word, as you will tend to read your speech rather than speaking directly to the audience. Instead, organize your speech in point-form notes, which you can quickly refer to during your presentation on The Big Day (try to make each point a kind of "trigger" for each thought, so you will talk to the audience in your own words rather than reading word-for-word from prepared text. I have included a sample of this technique later in the book).

When you rehearse your presentation, try to listen to how it sounds. Is it warm and conversational, or stiff and pompous? Are your sentences short and punchy, or long and cumbersome? Is there a nice flow to your delivery, or does it sound choppy and disorganized? Make sure the words you choose come across effectively to your audience.

Also be sure to write down the full names of everyone you will be called upon to introduce – it can be really embarrassing to go blank on the name of someone you're about to introduce (I forgot the name of a close friend's brother at a reception I emceed, and he was rather insulted). Check the pronunciation of names as well – you wouldn't believe how many people mispronounce a name like "Haibeck" (high beck). If you risk saying someone's name wrong, spell it out phonetically and include that in your speaking notes (as above).

I like to write my speaking notes on index cards, for easy handling. I use a pencil, to allow for last-minute changes or deletions. After I have written out all my material, I then number the cards so that I can quickly put them back in order should I arrive at the podium and drop them. I find it also helps to put a heading on each card for easy reference "Toast to the Bride" or "Introduction of Bride's Father".

If you plan to be humorous in delivering your presentation, remember to keep it in good taste. The jokes you told at the groom's stag probably won't go over well with the bride's grandmother. If the content of a joke or story could prove particularly offensive to even one person in that audience, my advice is not to use it. Also remember to watch the actual language that you use in telling jokes or stories.

The best kind of humor to use, in my opinion, is anecdotal. People love to hear humorous stories about people they know, and there's probably a wealth of material at your disposal about the bride and groom, their families and others in the wedding party. Be careful not to resort to a lot of "inside" humor, though, that only a few people will understand and appreciate.

If possible, try to interview each member of the wedding party before the wedding takes place to get information on where they live and work, their family, hobbies, sports interests, relation to the bride and groom, etc. Use this information to introduce them to the audience during your head table introductions, and don't be afraid to have some fun with this material by embellishing it or telling a few tall tales.

But please remember to make a few self-deprecating remarks about yourself before cutting up someone else. As mentioned, if you start off by poking a little fun at yourself, people will be much more apt to appreciate your later efforts in teasing someone else. And try to mix in an equal amount of pleasantries about each person to help balance the scale of good taste.

The best kind of jokes to use for the occasion, in my experience, are one-liners. Those long, narrative jokes you tell over coffee with a few buddies can become incredibly difficult to pull off in front of a large audience, so keep it simple and upbeat. I've included a treasury of suggested one-liners and other toasting material at the back of this book; you might find them helpful in preparing your material.

Don't leave your preparations to the last minute; material that you put together on the day of the wedding won't be nearly as well-considered as what you prepare several weeks prior to the wedding. You will also avoid the additional stress of having to prepare your material – and yourself – during the final days before the wedding. Those days can be stressful enough without having to slog your way through a last minute speech or wedding toast.

Always remember that the wedding and reception are in honor of the bride and groom. They're the stars, not you. Don't embarrass yourself and others by trying to upstage them or resorting to crude attempts at humor. Leave that to Uncle Buck (our fictional character in the cartoons contained within this book).

And finally, I would strongly recommend that you encourage guests not to drink and drive. Guests should always enjoy themselves – but they should never get behind the wheel of a car after drinking alcohol. Ask them to either take a cab or to ask you for help in arranging a safe ride home.

*"There's nothing like a little liquid courage
to calm your nerves!"*

Dealing With Your Nervousness

I'll never forget the first time I was asked to be the emcee at a wedding. I was working as a radio announcer at the time and had hosted numerous public events and receptions.

But when an old friend from high school called to ask if I would emcee his wedding, I agreed – and then began to shake in my boots. The ham in me could hardly wait to get in front of that microphone, but the chicken in me began to cluck about all kinds of imagined disasters.

For starters, I had no real idea of what was expected of me as emcee (I wish I'd had a book like this one). And I began to think of all the things that could possibly go wrong, from blowing my lines to forgetting people's names to passing out in front of the assembled guests.

It seems there's a world of difference between addressing a room full of strangers and a room full of your friends, family and peers. Perhaps it's the familiarity that can be so disconcerting – they know you and will continue to know you long after the wedding is over. If you blow it, they'll always be around to remind you of your moment of embarrassment.

On the other hand, you may never find a more supportive audience. These people presumably have some good feelings about you and are on your side. They'll understand that the wedding isn't a full-blown Hollywood production and will gladly laugh with you at your own mistakes. So don't take yourself too seriously; keep your cool and your sense of humor. Here are some tips that I've found helpful in dealing with my nervousness before a wedding:

Remember that it's normal to be nervous before speaking in public. Some of the world's greatest actors and orators are regularly reduced to jelly before "going on," at which time they reclaim their calm and perform marvelously.

Why? Because they have learned to use their nervous energy in sharpening their delivery, and focusing their concentration on the task at hand. If you're not somewhat nervous about your presentation, it may be a sign that you're inadequately prepared, and taking too casual an attitude towards your duties.

Put the job in perspective. You're simply being asked to preside over a wedding reception, not an international panel on nuclear-arms reduction. Ask yourself: What's the worst thing that could go wrong at this event?

I always imagine that the absolute worst thing that could happen to me is that I will lose all self-confidence, break down in tears in front of the crowd, and have to run out of the room. Having imagined that scenario, I am always comforted to realize that's all I'm really afraid of – embarrassing myself in front of some friends.

I'll still live to play another game of golf, enjoy many more fine dinners with my family, and read a lot more good books. By putting the job in perspective and confronting my own worst fears about it, I always come to the realization that life will still go on, even if I fail. That tends to reduce the pressure I may be feeling and boosts my confidence in going forward.

Do your homework. While a few lucky souls can speak brilliantly right off the cuff, most of us need to spend some time thinking about what we're going to say. That includes professional speakers, politicians, actors, comedians and talk show hosts. By following through with the tasks outlined in this book, you'll walk into that wedding feeling the kind of confidence that comes from being thoroughly prepared and ready to do your best.

Practice your delivery. Having thought about what you're going to say, now practice what you're going to say. I recommend you practice your presentation aloud several times to get a feel for how it sounds and to become comfortable with your delivery. You might also ask a friend or family member to listen to your presentation and to offer feedback on how it sounds.

Visualize your success. Many of the world's top golfers spend time before each round visualizing their success on the golf course. They go to a quiet place, close their eyes and see themselves driving the ball 300 yards, pitching to within a few feet of the cup, and rolling in a crisp putt to make birdie. These golfers have learned to program their subconscious mind to record "success patterns," and it works.

I suggest you try the same thing: Once you have prepared your presentation and rehearsed it a few times, try this exercise. Sit or lie down in a darkened room, take a few deep breaths, and try to relax your entire body. Then imagine yourself in front of the audience, speaking with confidence and enjoying your moment in the spotlight.

Run through your presentation in your mind's eye and visualize your success in delivering that presentation. Try to feel the glow of the audience as they warm to your delivery. See their smiling faces. Hear their laughter. Experience the burst of applause following your talk. Feel the pride – and the sense of relief – as you smile and walk back to your seat. Repeat this practice before you go to bed for at least five days prior to the reception.

View the room where the reception will be held. Make an appointment with the catering manager or whoever is responsible for the room in which the reception will be held and take a good look at the room. I like to do this several weeks in advance, if possible. This helps me get a clear picture of how the reception will unfold and aids in the visualization exercises I've described.

Rehearse in the room where the reception will be held. Students who experience anxiety about taking exams are often counseled to study in the room in which the examination will be given to help them develop a level of comfort with that environment. Apply the same technique to your situation. It will also help you get a feel for the acoustics of the room (but bear in mind that the acoustics will change once the room is full of people).

Video-tape your presentation. This can be a very powerful tool to help you improve your speaking and overall presentation skills. It will give you a much better sense of how you come across to the audience, and enable you to better identify both your strengths and your weaknesses.

But a word of caution: I only recommend that you do this if you are: a) relatively comfortable before the camera; b) able to effectively process and make use of that visual and auditory feedback in time for the wedding; c) committed to keeping your clothes on throughout the entire process (we don't need another one of "those" video-tapes making the rounds).

Some people react very negatively to seeing or hearing themselves on tape (especially if they're naked). If they are working with a professional speaking coach who can lead them through that process and help them deal with their anxiety and continue to hone their speaking abilities, they can achieve break-through success.

But if you video-tape yourself and wind up being totally freaked out by the size of your nose, the shrill pitch of your voice and the flailing manner of your hand gestures, you will probably carry that self-consciousness right into the reception.

Case in point: Many years ago, I won a video camera at a golf tournament. I was playing exceptionally well at the time, and felt very comfortable with my swing. Guess what happened? I used the camera to record my swing – and was astonished to learn that it didn't look at all how I had envisioned! I spent the next few months thinking more about fixing my swing instead of just hitting the ball, and it took a half dozen lessons to get me back on track.

Do some physical exercise on the day of the wedding. Go for a run, a walk, or a good swim on them morning of the wedding to help burn off some of your nervous energy. That exercise will also fuel your body with fresh oxygen and feed your brain with endorphins (those chemicals that produce the famed "natural high" that runners get following a good work-out). As a result, you will head into the events of The Big Day feeling more relaxed, healthy and clear (you'll also look better with those ruddy cheeks and bulging biceps).

Don't drink until after your program is finished. Many people like to loosen up with a few drinks before making a presentation, but I would strongly discourage you from doing so in your role as emcee or best man. One or two drinks might be OK for a lot of people, but to go beyond that is to invite trouble. You are in charge – and you need to have a clear head and your wits about you in presiding over that event.

You might also encourage others who will be called upon to speak or make a toast to minimize their drinking prior to "going on." Most of us have been to a wedding that has featured the slurred, rambling speech of a drunken best man or an inebriated father of the bride – and it can be downright embarrassing for everyone involved.

Another case in point: At the time of this writing, a story has made headlines around the world about a marriage gone awry following a drunken toast at a wedding reception. According to a report that was first published in the London Daily Telegraph, a Manchester couple's marriage lasted all of 90 minutes following the groom's drunken – and apparently highly inappropriate – toast to the bridesmaids. Enraged, the bride reportedly hit the groom over the head with an ashtray, which prompted an ugly brawl that sent the groom to jail and the bride to a divorce lawyer.

While that's obviously a very extreme case, it's not at all unusual for an alcohol-induced rant to ruin an otherwise wonderful wedding.

Further, given the fact that you have been given the responsibility of hosting and taking charge of the wedding reception on behalf of the couple, you need to take the role seriously and to fulfill those responsibilities with dignity and grace. Believe me, you will be much more likely to do so in a sober state (such as Utah).

I would also suggest you drink sparingly the night before the wedding; again, speaking from experience, there's nothing worse than being horribly hung over while trying to take charge of a wedding. We partied until the wee hours the night prior to the first wedding I was ever asked to emcee, and I can attest to the difficulties of trying to rise to the occasion when you're fighting to keep down your dinner. So put a cork in the bottle and give yourself a curfew the night before the wedding – you will be glad you did when it's time to take centre stage.

Do some relaxation exercises before the reception. I like to spend some time just after the wedding ceremony, and right before the reception, doing some relaxation exercises (and no, I don't mean pumping back a half-dozen martinis). There are plenty of books and tapes that can teach you various relaxation techniques, and I find them very helpful in controlling my nervousness.

Do some deep breathing. Just prior to your presentation, concentrate on taking several slow, deep breaths to relax your entire body. Take a few more deep breaths as you rise and approach the podium, position the microphone and lay down your notes. Continue to breathe as you address the audience.

Look for kind eyeballs in the audience. There are always certain people in an audience who will smile at you and listen attentively to what you are saying. Find those people early in your presentation and speak to them as much as you can. I've even gone so far in some presentations as to ask friends or family members in the audience to play a conscious role in offering those kindly eyes.

Remember that your audience empathizes with you. Nearly everyone has experienced some sort of embarrassing moment as a public speaker and can therefore relate to the nervousness you may be feeling. As a matter of fact, according to numerous surveys, public speaking ranks as the number one fear of the greatest number of people – ranking ahead of death by fire! You are by no means alone should you share that fear.

Acknowledge your fear. Sometimes it helps to actually tell your audience that you're feeling nervous – in effect, to get it off your chest. Don't dwell on it – just smile and tell the audience *"I'm a tad nervous right now, so please bear with me."* An admission like that demonstrates both your humility and your humanity – and your audience will relate to your feelings as such. Try to also remember that the audience wants you to succeed. They're pulling for you and they want to enjoy your presentation.

Don't be afraid to laugh at yourself. Comedians like Jay Leno and Bob Newhart get some of their best laughs when they blow a routine and make fun of themselves for doing so. Have a good laugh at yourself, if necessary. It will break the ice and help you to release some anxiety in the process.

Study the pros. I recently attended a live taping of *The Late Show with David Letterman.* It was fabulous! I haven't laughed that hard in years, and the experience of watching Letterman get goofy with his guests, mug for the cameras, toy with the audience and kibitz with his band was something I'll never forget. It was educational, inspiring and a joy to watch – and those of us who are inclined towards performing tend to internalize and play off that kind of experience – just like a tennis fanatic becomes a better player by watching the pros. So go to a comedy club, an improv performance or a funny play and get into the spirit of live performance.

Take a course or join a Toastmasters group. I can't say enough about the value of breaking through your fear of public speaking. It's always amazed me how kindergarten students can stand up in front of their classmates and deliver the most unabashed speeches about the items they bring for "show and tell." But somewhere along the road to adulthood, many of us lose that confidence and become terrified of speaking to an audience.

I was such a specimen. In my youth, I could address a radio audience with relative ease, but when faced with that same audience live and in person, I could hardly utter my name, let alone a coherent speech.

That changed with my enrollment in the Dale Carnegie Course (www.dalecarnegie.com). My life was quite literally transformed (at the tender age of 19), as I mastered my fear of public speaking and gained a confidence that extended into every area of my life. Millions of other graduates will attest to that same experience, and I highly recommend it to anyone who has a fear of public speaking. Toastmasters also offers some excellent training and speaker development programs (see www.toastmasters.org).

*"Why, I've known the bride so long,
I met her even before she was a virgin."*

Some Tips on Making Toasts

At some weddings, the emcee will simply introduce people who are going to make toasts, rather than making any themselves. If the emcee is also the best man, however, toasting is part of the territory. Ditto in the case of the maid of honor acting as emcee, or someone else close to the wedding couple (a friend or relative).

But regardless of whether the emcee is expected to make a toast or not, he or she is often asked for advice (from others in the wedding party) on how to write and deliver an effective toast.

The best advice I can offer is to keep the toast short and simple, and to bear in mind that it is ultimately intended to be a tribute to the person being toasted. That doesn't mean you can't throw in a few good-natured barbs along the way to that tribute – more on that later – but don't make the mistake (as I once did) of turning that celebratory wedding toast into a Don Rickles roast. Remember, this is the wedding part – not the bachelors at the bar part.

I would also like to offer that far too many people, in my experience, strive to become someone they're not in making a toast. Quoting flowery passages from famous speeches or poems, they try to emulate the oratory excellence of a Lincoln or a Churchill and wind up sounding like a pompous, stuffed shirt.

Better, in my opinion, to just be yourself and employ the same tactic I've covered in applying humor to your presentation – that is, use anecdotal material about the person or persons to whom you are toasting. As the individual chosen for this task, you are probably very familiar with the background and character of the bride, or the groom, or whomever is being toasted; use that information to make a warm, personalized toast.

At our wedding, the person who made the toast to the bride was a close friend of my wife's family. He told a few humorous stories about her when she was a little girl and then related how he had watched her grow up to become the mature, sophisticated woman she is today. It was a very moving toast, made simply and from the heart.

That's the kind of speech audiences love to hear at a wedding reception. It's an emotional day for all concerned, and people have a right to be sentimental as they celebrate the day. But bear in mind that balance is also important – in the same way that some people sometimes go too far in trying to be funny, other people can get carried away with the schmaltzy stuff. Ditto for religious diatribes – I once attended a wedding at which the father of the groom decided to deliver a thirty-minute+ speech on spirituality as part of his wedding toast. A short prayer or recital of a brief religious passage may be appropriate, but save us all from the Saturday night sermons.

While on that subject, I want to clarify what I said earlier on the concept of using famous quotations. Using a quotation from a famous person can indeed be an effective platform upon which to build a speech. But again, just don't overdo it. I've heard people try to weave together a dozen or more of these lofty statements into a wedding speech, and the result is usually the same. They sound phony and over the top. Better, in my opinion, to take one key quote and use that as an opening upon which to craft your speech.

Be yourself. If you're a fairly serious individual, make a serious toast. Don't try to be funny if you're not a funny person. If you are, by all means inject some lighthearted material into your presentation. In short, let your comments and delivery reflect your own individual style and personality. Be sincere – and as a famous playwright once wrote, *"to thine own self be true."*

If you do decide to make a humorous speech as part of your toast, remember to conclude it on a more serious, upbeat note that honors the recipient of the toast. For example, if the balance of your speech recounts a series of humorous traits or misadventures of the groom, be sure to end it with some sincere praise for the groom. Talk about why you admire him, what his friendship has meant to you, why he will make an excellent partner for his new bride and how much you'll miss him now that he's married (OK, maybe you'd better skip the last part).

Choose a theme for your toast (I've included a separate chapter on this topic). You might build your talk around a tribute to the bride; advice on keeping a marriage strong and happy; the meaning of love; the special interests of the bride and groom; or a rollicking account of how they met and became engaged (and by the way, I think it makes sense to acknowledge the groom as part of any toast to the bride – and vice versa).

A toast need never be longer than ten minutes, in my opinion. Unless the speaker is exceptionally good, the audience will quickly lose interest beyond that point. As a general rule of thumb, I would encourage people to try to make their toast between three to five minutes (or less). You might also suggest that people making toasts consider timing themselves while rehearsing their speech, to help develop a feel for the length of their presentation.

When making your toast, maintain eye contact with your audience and look around the room so everyone feels included. Also be sure to occasionally look at the person to whom you're giving the toast to help focus attention on that individual. That will honor the person you are toasting, and take some of the pressure off you while you're making the toast.

Some people make brilliant speeches leading up to their toast and then seem unsure what to say in proposing the actual toast. Remember that the conclusion of a toast is like a call to action. After delivering your speech, ask people to rise (if they are seated). Give them plenty of time to do so. Then focus your attention on the subject of the toast, raise your glass and ask people to join with you in drinking to the new bride/the new couple/the bridesmaids or whomever. *"Ladies and gentlemen, please join me in a toast to the Bride"* or *"Ladies and gentlemen, to the Bride and Groom."* Take a small sip of your beverage, smile again at the subject of the toast and then return to your seat.

A word of advice on the standing-up part: If there are to be multiple toasts at the wedding reception, and people are seated, you should probably avoid asking guests to rise for each toast. That process will get tiresome – and for elderly people (or those who have joined Uncle Buck in his whiskey taste-testing spree), it can be difficult to repeatedly rise from their table and stand to participate in a toast. If that is the case, simply conclude your toast with a brief pause (count one, two, three), turn and smile at the recipient of the toast, then say: *"Ladies and gentlemen, please join me ... in raising your glasses ... as we salute the marriage of Bob & Carol"* (or some version of that).

And dumb as it sounds, remember to bring your glass with you if you are called to the podium to make a toast. It's downright embarrassing to make your brilliant speech and then suddenly realize you have no glass to raise in concluding your toast (somehow an "air toast" just doesn't have the same effect). Use a wine glass or champagne flute, even if you're drinking juice or soda. A great toast deserves to be made with a decent glass.

Some other dumb mistakes to avoid: If it's the bride and/or groom's second marriage, don't mention their first marriage. Believe it or not, people can be a little sensitive about their first failed attempt at marital bliss. If it's their third or fourth, however, go for it – they're sure to have developed a sense of humor about it all by then. Don't get into any embarrassing speculation about their honeymoon or the recreational opportunities they might pursue behind closed doors. Avoid any references to the bride's weight, shoe size, past boyfriends or her recent appearance on the Jerry Springer Show. And remember that it's very poor etiquette to try to toast and chew gum at the same time (seriously – ditch the gum).

As for the order of wedding toasts, it's fairly typical for the best man to offer the first toast, which is usually to the bride and/or new couple. After that, the fathers might offer their own tribute to the new bride or groom or the new couple (although another option is to take care of that at the rehearsal dinner). The groom might then respond, as may the bride.

The maid of honor could also be included, as could other family members, friends, parents and anyone else who would like to offer a toast to the new couple. At some weddings, the pre-arranged series of toasts are followed by an "open microhone" session at which anyone present is invited to offer a toast or tell a favorite story about the bride and groom. That can be a lot fun – but take a careful read on your audience before going there. If they're well into their cups and teetering towards oblivion, an open microphone can be an open invitation to disaster.

The actual subjects of wedding toasts are typically: the bride or groom as individuals; the bride and groom as a couple; the bridesmaids; the bride's parents; the best man; and special guests. Bear in mind, though, that there is no legal requirement or societal bylaw that demands such an order of toasts, or that all of those individuals be toasted. Do what works for you and your family – it's your wedding, and it needn't be complicated by an obsession with etiquette. If you prefer a more relaxed, spontaneous approach, go for it!

But for now, back to Etiquette 101 – "How to Properly Receive a Toast." Contrary to what often happens, those being toasted do not participate in the actual toast. They do not stand or raise their glasses or sip their drink – they should simply smile and nod back at the audience with a gracious "*Thank You!*" They are not obliged to make a toast in return.

And a final note to emcees: If the person who has just made a toast has been particularly humorous, don't try to upstage his or her performance with your own comedy bit at that point. The audience will need a bit of a rest and you will be better received with a more understated approach. Simply thank the person and move on to the next part of the program.

"I'm sure you're all aware these two have been sleeping together for years..."

Inspirational Themes for a Wedding Toast

Remember how your Grade Ten teacher harped at you about the need to develop a specific theme for your essay? Well, guess what: The same principle applies to writing an effective speech.

Good speechwriters know that an audience can only grasp a limited amount of information at any one sitting – and thus one of the best ways to grab and hold their attention is by throwing out a theme statement and structuring your talk around that.

If you have access to the Internet, log on and consider a few of history's greatest speeches:

- **Winston Churchill** rallying a nation around a theme of *"We Shall Never Surrender"* (www.usnews.com/usnews/news/churchill/box.htm);

- **Martin Luther King** inspiring social reform with his famous speech *"I Have a Dream"* (www.mecca.org/~crights/dream.html);

- **President John F. Kennedy's** stirring inaugural speech with his famous appeal: *"Ask not what your country can do for you — ask what you can do for your country!"* (www.bartleby.com/124/pres56.html).

Now certainly no wedding speech or toast need be as serious or dramatic as any of those examples. But in the same way that those speeches were written around a central theme – and given life through the insertion of brilliant analogies, colorful metaphors and the use of short, crisp sentences – so too can your wedding speech benefit from those same time-honored principles.

Communicating with an audience at a wedding reception has particular challenges. Many guests may be experiencing a degree of *"attention-deficit-disorder-through-the-effects-of-an-alcoholic-surplus syndrome"* – resulting in a certain degree of difficulty in following the spoken word. (The good news is that they may be more inclined to find humor in your lame jokes and droll one-liners). Make it easy for them to tune into your toast by keeping it simple (and perhaps short).

The other major reason why I think it makes sense to build your toast around a theme is that it helps you to stay focused in writing and delivering it. Being asked to make a wedding toast is a great honor, but for many people, it can also be a source of tremendous anxiety: What should I say? How do I organize my talk? How do I hold people's attention?

By choosing a theme, you will immediately begin to hone in on what you want to say. You will have a consistent body of thought from which to draw your inspirations and organize your key points. And when it comes time to deliver your toast, you will do so with greater confidence, knowing that your speech is going to follow a clear-cut, well-defined path of information that will be easy for your audience to follow.

Let me give you an example. One of the all-time best wedding speeches I've ever witnessed was at the wedding of my brother-in-law.

His best man delivered a toast that quite literally had the audience in hysterics with his account of *"Growing Up with the Groom."* He told us of their mischievous childhood pranks, their outrageous competition for girlfriends, their ineptitude in waiting tables together in a restaurant, and their buffoonery in sinking a sailboat (they apparently forgot about the tide one night when they dropped anchor).

He concluded with a few earnest thoughts about what their life-long friendship had meant to him, and offered that if the prevailing force in any good marriage is a solid friendship between husband and wife – then theirs would endure a lifetime, for John (the groom) had indeed proven to be an exceptional friend.

It was simple, enlightening, humorous and consistent. And the audience loved it!

Another key element of that speech was the fact that it was made from the heart – and based upon some very real human experience. As mentioned, I believe that anecdotal stories are the best source of material for a wedding toast or speech. Any speaker becomes far more eloquent with the re-telling of a story that he or she has personally experienced. And the audience at a wedding reception loves to hear those kind of humorous, real-life stories (providing they are in reasonably good taste).

You were there – you saw him or her sink the sailboat or drop the hot bowl of soup on the customer's lap – and as a result, you will tell those stories in your own words, and in a far more real and compelling manner than you would in telling a joke (that's because a joke typically involves the re-telling of a made-up story that has no real connection to you; most jokes also rely on superb timing to make the punch-line work, and most people have difficulty with that before a large audience).

I've also noticed over the years that most people tend to automatically become more animated and amused in the re-telling of their own stories. They begin to smile and laugh as the memories emerge, and the audience tends to laugh along with them. The lampooned groom begins to blush and squirm; his new bride shrieks with every new twist to the outrageous tale; his family and friends are hysterical with the shared memory of it all; and the new in-laws start to feel better about the guy marrying into their family, knowing he's a bit of a doofus.

Bear in mind, though, that humor doesn't HAVE to be a part of any wedding toast or speech; if you're not a particularly humorous person or your subject matter doesn't easily lend itself to humor, go with the more earnest approach.

So having said all that, here are nine proven themes for you to consider in building your wedding toast or speech:

- **Friendship** – What do you remember most about your experience with the bride, the groom or the party being toasted? What happened that was funny? What did you learn from your friendship? What makes this person such a good friend? How will that demonstrated history of friendship translate into a promising marriage?

- **How They Met** – People at a wedding reception also love to hear stories about how the couple met, their courtship, how and where The Big Question was popped, wedding jitters, etc. You can have a lot of fun with this one ("Contrary to popular belief, Bob did *not* meet Carol while visiting his relatives at the county zoo."

- **Watching Them Grow** – For an older person who has personally witnessed the growth of a younger person (uncle; aunt; grandparent; neighbor; minister; parole officer), there may be a wealth of fascinating material to share with the audience about your observations on things like their birth, early childhood, education, first jobs, old flames, new hairpiece.

- **Prescription for a Successful Marriage** – We can all benefit from words of wisdom about what it takes to build and sustain a happy marriage. You might tackle this on the basis of your own experience or through researching the subject matter with someone you know that has a long and particularly good marriage.

- **The Somewhat Exaggerated Biographical Sketch** – This one works well if you are asked to make a Toast to the Bridesmaids (or other people in the wedding party whom you don't know that well). Interview the person(s) prior to the reception (a few weeks ahead is better than five minutes prior) and find out what they do, where they live, if they are married or single, what their hobbies are, pet peeves, worst experiences, etc. and then embellish some of those facts in your toast. Have fun with it – but keep it in (relatively) good taste.

- **A Toast to Love & Laughter & Happily Ever-After** – If you wish to keep your toast short and sweet, you might simply offer your sincere wishes for the new couple to live a life together based on the above. That's also a great theme to use in discussing the new couple's relationship and in wishing them a happy future together.

- **Famous Quotations** – These are my least favorite form of toasts because they lack the personalized and more experiential qualities of those described above. But it you're not comfortable making a speech or telling a story, citing the wise words of others can prove both informative and entertaining for your audience. Here's a few samples; there are many more in the back of the book.

"May you grow old together on one pillow."
– Armenian Proverb

"Never above you. Never below you. Always beside you."
– Walter Winchell

"The greatest of all arts is the art of living together."
– William Lyon Phelps

A final thought on content for your speech or toast: As any good presenter knows, visuals can be a highly effective means to reinforce key points and keep your audience involved. Why not apply the same techniques to your presentation at the wedding?

By using a software program such as PowerPoint (you're welcome, Mr. Gates), you can put together a series of pictures and text to tell the life story of the person(s) you are honoring. Start with those embarrassing baby pictures and then progress through the rest of their life, using the occasional text slide to transition into new eras or to inject humorous asides.

For some truly brilliant examples of transition slides, have a look at some old re-runs of the *"Frasier"* show; the creative team used a sharp black screen to frame the clever headlines (in white text) that introduced each new scene, and the effect was often hilarious.

A SAMPLE SPEECH BY THE BEST MAN

Here's the full text version of a speech I once gave when asked to serve as the best man. The point form version follows – and that's the one I would have used as a reference tool at the reception itself. I have written this one out word for word in order to give you a better feel for its content and how it would sound when delivered.

The theme for the speech is friendship. It is similar to the one I have just described in the previous chapter – and again, the audience loved it. They learned some things about the groom that they hadn't known before – again, wedding guests love to know more about the people involved in the event. They also had a good laugh along the way.

Note the crisp, short sentences. That makes them a lot easier to deliver. Also note the areas where I would pause – timing is everything in life, especially when you're trying to be funny or attempting to emphasize a key thought.

Please also note the fact that I have interspersed some positive observations about the groom amongst my many gentle barbs about our history. In our case, we have always enjoyed a lot of kibitzing back and forth, so it was certainly fitting for me to rib him a bit at his wedding. But I also wanted to recognize some of his positive attributes and accomplishments (despite how difficult they were to identify). The speech concludes with a few heartfelt thoughts about our life-long friendship.

A Toast to the Groom

Harry and I met while we were in kindergarten. He was the skinny kid with the glasses and big feet.

I remember him well. When the teacher used to ask us what we wanted to be when we grew up, most of us would reply that we wanted to become a fireman or a cowboy or an astronaut.

But not Harry. He'd stand up and proclaim: "I want to be an Attorney at Law, practicing civil litigation."

I swear he said that. He was a guy who always knew what he wanted in life. While other kids were out playing baseball, he was studying the history of torts.

Harry's mastery of the law came in handy a few years later when he filed a claim against our Grade Three teacher for unlawful confinement. She laughed so hard she actually let us out a few minutes early from the detention she had given us.

His childhood hero was Howard Cosell. I'm serious. Howard Cosell! Harry liked the fact that he knew so much about sports ... that he was argumentative ... and that he was a lawyer!

It's said that our childhood heroes often have a bearing on who we become as adults. In Harry's case, that's certainly true. He's insufferable with his knowledge of sports. Totally argumentative. And of course, he's a lawyer.

By the way, does anyone know how to save a drowning lawyer? (pause). Good!

Anyway, as I mentioned, Harry always seemed to know what he wanted. He was our Class Valedictorian in Grade Nine. He made the football team ... and the basketball team ... despite his hopelessly limited athletic ability. Even more amazing was the fact that he managed to get a girl to go out with him that year.

High school was another matter. As always, Harry excelled in school. And he continued to make the most of his meager athletic abilities. But something very fundamental about him changed in Grade Ten. Something that took us all by surprise ... and changed his life ... forever.

Harry discovered the magic of ... contact lenses! Yes, our former four-eyed friend lost his Coke bottle glasses and nerdy demeanor. It was kind of like Clark Kent going into the phone booth. He became someone totally new.

In Harry's case, that new persona was to become ... well, I was going to say "chick magnet" but that would be stretching it. Let's just say he suddenly hit the radar screens of a few desperate teenaged girls.

He also managed to hit a lot of walls. Literally! His transition from Coke bottle glasses to Coke bottle lenses wasn't without its challenges for Harold, and he managed to run smack into his share of walls that year.

And we'll never forget the day he mistakenly made his way into the Girl's locker room. Or at least, he claimed it was a mistake!

Anyway, Harry managed to hit his share of books as well, and he graduated with first-class honors from high school.

College was next. He earned a Degree in Commerce ... along with several scholarships. He also earned the title of "Designated Drinker" in the residence building where he lived.

To cap his academic achievements, Harry was accepted into one the top law schools in this country. He was apparently the only applicant in the history of that school to submit a resume starting from the time he was in kindergarten ... and included the decision by our Grade Three teacher to reduce our sentence.

As we all know, Harold met his future Bride-to-be at law school. And over the next three years, he discovered a part of life that proved to be even more interesting than the law. He found love.

He and Carol became insufferable ... I mean, inseparable. They sat together. Studied together. Ate together. And began to wear matching hot pink outfits together. They were truly adorable.

And they look adorable here, today ... even if they're not still wearing hot pink. But in all seriousness, Harry is one of my oldest and best friends. He's like a brother to me ... and we've been through a lot together.

Through those years, he's always been there for me. And I know he will always be there for Carol.

Ladies & gentlemen, I would like to invite you to rise ... and to join with me ... in offering a toast ... to our dear friend, Harry ... and his beautiful new bride!

Have a look at the next page to see a point-form version of that same speech. Note how I've used single words or phrases to trigger my thoughts about what I want to say. That allows for a coherent order of thoughts, delivered in a much more natural style than reading the speech word-for-word from a prepared text. Try it -- you'll find it allows for a much more natural delivery.

Toast to the Groom

- Kindergarten. Glasses. Big Feet.
- Fireman. Cowboy. Astronaut.
- Attorney at Law/Civil Litigation.

- Swear he said that. Out playing baseball. History of Torts.
- Unlawful confinement. Sprung us loose from detention.

- Hero – Howard Cosell.
- Sports. Argue. Lawyer.
- Childhood heroes. Insufferable. Argumentative. Lawyer.
- Drowning lawyer? Good!

- Valedictorian. Football/basketball – despite limited athletic ability.
- Even more amazing. Got girl to go out with him.

- High school. Excelled.
- Made most of meager athletic ability.
- Fundamental change. Took us all by surprise.
- Discovered magic of – contact lenses!

- Former four-eyed friend.
- Lost Coke bottle lenses/nerdy demeanor.
- Clark Kent going into phone booth.
- Chick magnet. Hit radar screens. Also walls.

- Hit books – honors.
- Commerce Degree. Designated drinker.

- Top law school. Resume from kindergarten. Reduce our sentence.
- Met Bride-to-be.

- Even more interesting than the law. Love.
- He & Carol became insufferable/inseparable.
- Sat together. Studied. Ate. Hot pink. Adorable.

- Adorable today. No hot pink.
- One of oldest & best friends. Brother.
- Been through a lot together.

- Always been there. Will be for Carol.
- Toast to the Groom/beautiful new Bride!

"Test, test, test, testicle...oops, too loud eh?"

Delivering Your Presentation

You've reached zero hour. The wedding is over, and the reception is beginning. Guests are mingling easily, and everyone seems very happy. The bride looks radiant; the groom looks terrified; and their parents look ashen, as they mentally calculate the costs of this gala affair.

If you have done your homework to this point, you will be feeling very good about the situation. Everything is under control, and you are in charge. You have rehearsed your presentation and feel comfortable with your material. You are well-acquainted with a carefully planned agenda. And you're excited about what promises to be a truly memorable evening.

Check with the bride or her mother for any last minute changes you should know about. Reassure them and let them know that everything is moving along as planned. Have a quick word with the catering manager (or whomever your contact is) to make sure everything is running smoothly on their end. And seek out the band leader or disc jockey (if they are present) to touch base and review the evening's agenda.

While people are still mingling and going through the receiving line, take a few moments to check the public address system, if there is one. Simply turn on the microphone and count to four, or say "test ... test ... test" (you know the drill). Be sure to do this, though, as you'll get off to a bad start if the P.A. system lets you down.

Better still to check the sound before people arrive at the reception hall – that way, if there is a problem, you will have more time to get it fixed and your experimentation with it won't interrupt the reception. Remember that the acoustics will change when the room is full of people, so be prepared to project your voice into the microphone a bit more.

Also remember to hold the microphone somewhere between three to ten inches away from you and slightly below your mouth (microphones are all a bit different, so if at all possible, try to experiment with the one you will be using before the event). If the microphone is attached to a lectern, be sure to raise or lower the mike so that it's positioned about a foot away from you. Speak directly into the microphone and hold it steady. Try not to sway or bob about, as your voice will fade in and out. Speak in your normal voice – there's no need to shout, as the microphone will naturally amplify your voice.

As you stand and walk to the podium (or upon reaching the podium), try smiling at the audience before saying anything. You'll be amazed at what a sincere smile can do in winning people over from the start. This is, after all, a happy occasion, and your audience will literally mirror your smile back at you.

There will most likely be a lectern for you to use (if there isn't, ask for one before the guests arrive). Use the lectern to spread your agenda and speaking notes in front of you, with the agenda printed on a single piece of paper and your speaking notes on the numbered index cards. Lay your watch next to the agenda so that you will be able to refer to it in a more discreet manner. And make sure you have a pen or pencil with you to make last minute changes or to jot down new thoughts.

Keep a glass of water handy should you need to clear your throat; I usually also have a throat lozenge or two before going on. If you really want to get professional about your vocal quality, gargle with some warm salt water just before the start of your presentation (preferably in the washroom). Avoid drinking ice-cold beverages, as they will constrict your vocal chords. I prefer to drink warm water or hot tea before and during a speaking engagement of any kind. Speaking of beverages, remember to have a glass of wine, champagne or a soft drink handy for toasts. The beverage you choose should be poured into a proper wine or champagne glass prior to your toast.

As described in the section about preparing an agenda, I've found that the best way to start your presentation is to arrange for a rousing welcome for the new couple (and perhaps the head table). That way, you can break the ice with a simple statement – *"Good evening, ladies and gentlemen – and welcome. My name is _____, and I will be your Master of Ceremonies for this evening. Please join me in welcoming the new Mr. & Mrs. _____!* (lead applause).

The room will immediately come to life (through the applause given to the new couple), attention will immediately re-focus from you to the bride and groom, and the celebration will be underway!

Once the couple is seated, you can then make a few more simple announcements about dinner and the evening to follow, introduce the person who is to offer the blessing and then take your seat and relax. That simple process will enable you to shake off those pre-event jitters while generating some immediate warmth and energy in the room itself.

Make sure you have something to eat during dinner – you will need the energy for later on. Keep your body hydrated and your throat muscles relaxed by continuing to drink some warm water or tea during dinner. Do not drink more than a glass of wine at dinner. Better still, don't drink at all.

Skim through your speaking notes during dinner to refresh your mind about what you're going to say. If your notes are on index cards, you can easily store them in your jacket pocket. You might also want to carry a few extra copies of the agenda with you in case you need to give one to the caterer or the DJ or the bandmaster or anyone else involved in the reception festivities.

Start things off after dinner with a breezy welcome back (*"Hello again, and welcome to the second half of our show."*) Then re-introduce yourself (*"In case you've forgotten, I'm your host for this evening ......"*).

Read some humorous e-mails (don't be afraid to make a few up) and acknowledge the out-of-town guests and perhaps the more senior members of the respective families – grandparents,

---

elderly aunts and uncles, children over the age of 30 who are still living with their parents.

Again, pardon me for being so calculating, but I know how hard it can be for people to stand up before an audience and find a level of comfort in being there. By following those steps (short re-intro, followed by audience intros and humorous e-mails), you will quickly get the evening rolling again. You will also re-focus attention from you to the audience themselves, and renew the room's energy through the applause given to the special guests. You will also find some easy humor in the reading of a few light-hearted e-mails sent from guests who couldn't attend (make up a few, if you have to).

Stand tall while you're speaking to the audience. As you chat with them, remember to look around to each part of the room (so everyone feels included). Add some energy to your voice, and try to smile as you talk. That smile will automatically come through in your voice. If you're more comfortable grabbing the microphone from the podium and walking around with it, go for it (but check in advance to make sure it's either a wireless mike or one that has plenty of cable attached to it).

Be gracious and warm. Lead the applause following the introduction of each new speaker. Welcome them to the stage or podium by shaking their hand or giving them a hug. Smile and laugh with them as they deliver their speech or make their toast. Encourage them with your silent prayers and kind eyeballs. Thank and acknowledge them for their efforts in making that brilliant toast or speech. Be prepared to help them if they're overwhelmed with the task or extremely nervous. And in the worst case, use your own judgment in giving someone "the hook" if they become exceedingly drunk, long-winded or obnoxious.

To conclude your presentation, remember to thank the bride and groom for giving you the honor of being Master of Ceremonies and/or Best Man. Wish them well, and invite people to enjoy the rest of the evening (you may also want to introduce the band, disc jockey, or any other entertainment booked for the evening).

So relax, have fun, and good luck! You're going to be sensational!

Duties of the Best Man

So what does a "Best Man" actually do? Well, if we go to the very essence of the role, it's to stand up at a wedding to support the man getting married, and to witness the vows between bride and groom.

The best man and the maid of honor are also typically required to sign the wedding license to attest that the marriage has, in fact, taken place.

But being a best man means much more than that. It is one of the greatest affirmations of friendship between men, and to be chosen for the role is one of life's great honors. It's a big deal – and aside from the significance of the designation itself, the role carries with it tremendous responsibility. Treat that role with the respect it deserves, and vow to be the best friend you can be to the groom as he walks his path to marriage.

Getting married is ranked as one of the most stressful events one can experience, and in most cases, the groom can use all the help he can get. In my opinion, the most important thing you can do in your role as best man is to simply "be there" for the guy taking his vows. In my case, the best man at our wedding played a crucial role in helping me prepare for the Big Day.

We talked regularly during the period leading up to the wedding, and he listened to my concerns and shared my excitement. He accompanied me to the various engagement parties given in our honor; made sure I survived the bachelor party I'll never remember; took me for a walk just prior to the wedding ceremony to get some fresh air and help ease my nerves; sat with me in the minister's office prior to the wedding and told jokes while I paced back and forth; and generally provided the kind of friendship and solid base of support one needs during a major life-changing event.

(He also called our hotel room at 3:00 a.m. on the night of the wedding to inquire about our progress in consummating the marriage, but that's a whole other story).

It is most often a close friend or brother who is asked to be the best man – although I've been to one wedding at which the groom's father served as best man and another where a female friend of the groom served in this role (she even wore a tuxedo, which was a cute touch. Her suggestion that we hold the bachelor party at a day spa got vetoed, however).

Now to the mechanics of the role. If we were to write a job description for the best man, it would describe a series of duties to be undertaken prior, during and after the wedding to help ensure everything proceeds smoothly. That job might include all or many of the responsibilities listed below (the duties vary somewhat, depending upon the type of wedding and the expectations of the couple and their families).

As with any organizational structure, it's critically important for people to understand their role and its range of responsibilities. This can get a little complicated if there is to be a best man AND an emcee for the wedding. Therefore, it's important that they review and agree upon their roles prior to the event in order to prevent confusion later.

Perhaps the best way to divide up responsibilities is to let the best man help the groom with arrangements leading up to the reception; the Master of Ceremonies can then take charge of the reception itself (with the bride's mother serving as chairman of the board, of course). The best man will make the Toast to the Groom at the wedding and perhaps help with some of the logistics, but the emcee should be empowered to host and oversee (on behalf of the bride and groom) the reception itself.

Here's a list of some of the official duties of a best man (as originally offered by Dear Abby and enhanced by yours truly):

- Volunteering to help the bride's mother or wedding organizers as needed;

- Accompanying the groom to the engagement parties and other events leading up to the wedding;

- Helping the groom coordinate the formal-wear fittings (if required) for others in the wedding party;

- Liaising with those other members of the wedding party to ensure they pay for their own formal-wear rental charges;

- Heading up the organizing committee for the bachelor party, including the collection of funds from the guests to pay for the party itself (the groom shouldn't have to bear any of those costs);

- Ensuring the safe transportation of all guests at the bachelor party (if liquor is to be involved);

- Stepping in as necessary to help ensure the groom doesn't endure too much abuse at the bachelor party (seriously, alcohol poisoning can be deadly, and to force the groom to drink shot after shot of alcohol is to invite serious consequences – or at least, a big mess to clean up);

- Either separately (or with the ushers) providing a special gift to the groom to help commemorate the event and the special friendship it involves (a framed picture of the group at the bachelor party, signed by all the guys, is a nice touch);

- Attending the rehearsal dinner and being available to help with any last minute arrangements for the wedding itself;

- Making the arrangements to transport the groom to the wedding (I would suggest you arrange to pick him up and drive him to the church);

- If necessary, helping the groom get dressed for the wedding (it's amazing how difficult those stupid tuxedo shirt button things can be to get done up when you're due to get married in an hour);

- Making sure the ushers have their proper attire and that they appear on time at the wedding ceremony;

- Instructing the ushers on the proper procedure for greeting guests and escorting them to their seats (family and friends of the bride on the left side of the church, family and friends of the groom on the right side);

- Presenting the clergy with the envelope containing the fee for the ceremony;

- Sitting with the groom prior to the wedding (the best man does not help with the ushering process). This can be one of *the* most stressful times of all for the groom, so plan to be there with him during his final moments of freedom ... I mean bachelorhood.

- Reviving the groom should he faint when the minister calls for you to head to the altar;

- Standing proud next to him during the wedding ceremony, acting as a witness to the vows and in the signing of the official marriage license;

- Taking possession of the wedding ring(s) prior to the ceremony, and providing them to the minister at the time during the ceremony that they are required;

- Ensuring a bottle of chilled champagne (or their beverage of choice) awaits the bride and groom in the limousine (or other mode of transportation) from the wedding ceremony to the reception hall;

- Mingling with the guests at the reception and being available to assist with last minute errands, announcements or other logistics as required;

- Riding shotgun with the groom during the reception and running interference should his new mother-in-law choose to offer her unsolicited opinion on his choice in wedding socks;

- Offering a Toast to the Groom or a first toast to the new couple;

- Breaking up any bar fights that might erupt between rival in-laws;

- Gathering up the wedding gifts and transporting them for safe storage;

- Helping the groom as needed in packing a vehicle, confirming hotel reservations, or driving the couple to the airport or hotel;

- Attending the gift-opening party the next day (if one is planned);

- Ensuring the ushers and other male members of the wedding party return their formal-wear rentals on time.

As you can see, the best man's responsibilities extend far beyond just showing up at the wedding and witnessing the vows. It is indeed a lot to take on – but it's also a tremendous honor to be asked to serve as best man. Bear that in mind – and know that your support will be critically important to the success of the wedding (and the mental health of the groom).

So go forward with honor and courage ... tackle your role with vigor and enthusiasm ... pledge to be there for your brother in his final hours ... make it your quest to help celebrate his wedding to the fullest ... and be the best, Best Man that you can be!

Oh, and don't forget to short-sheet his bed.

"A toast to the happy couple -- and their ability to put that whole ugly 'restraining order' business behind them!"

A Treasury of Wedding Toasts, Quotes & Humor

The following pages list dozens of suggested wedding toasts, one-liners and famous quotations for you to consider in preparing for your role as Master of Ceremonies (or to sprinkle into your wedding toast or speech).

Some are romantic. Others are philosophical. And many are satirical. Use them at your discretion – and please note that I have tried to provide a balance between the male and female-oriented subject matter.

Keep it light and remember how important it is to laugh at ourselves and to see the humor in life (including marriage). For just as Hollywood excess is a constant source of amusement at Academy Awards presentations, the wonders and eccentricities of marriage make for some great material at a wedding reception. Just remember to: a) know your audience; b) make fun of yourself first; c) say some nice things, too.

May your friendship endure in both sunshine and shade.

May you share a joy that grows deeper, a friendship that grows closer, and a marriage that grows richer through the years.

May the twinkle in your eyes stay with you, and the love in your hearts never fade.

May the love you share forever remain as beautiful as the bride looks today.

Do not marry a person that you know you can live with; only marry someone that you cannot live without.

Love is blind, but marriage can be a real eye-opener.

A rhetorical question only a married man can appreciate: If a man stands alone in the forest, and there are no women around to hear him speak, is he still wrong?

No one in love is free, or wants to be.

The most important thing in a relationship between a man and a woman is that one of them must be good at taking orders.

Success is getting what you want. Happiness is wanting what you get.

Once married, remember that the length of a minute depends on which side of a bathroom door you're standing on.

The most effective way to remember your spouse's birthday is to forget it once.

Some people are so determined to find blissful happiness that they overlook a lifetime of contentment.

There are some who feel it is inappropriate to make fun of the holy institution of marriage. Then there are others who know it's the only way we can live with it.

A good marriage is like a casserole; only those responsible for it really know what goes in it.

My wife only has two complaints. One, she has nothing to wear. Two, there's never enough space in her closet.

Marriage is the sole cause of divorce.

Marriage is the process of finding out what kind of person your spouse would have really preferred.

A husband is living proof that a wife can take a joke.

Number one tip for newlyweds: your mother-in-law is always right.

May all your ups and downs be between the sheets.

Remember: On any disagreement, the husband is always entitled to the last few words ... "Yes, dear."

Always remember that a woman has the last word in any argument. Anything a man says after that ... is the beginning of a new argument.

I can only hope that you will be as happy in life as me and "What's her name?"

Keep your eyes open before marriage – half shut afterwards.

Let there be spaces in your togetherness.

Marriage is a thing you've got to give your whole mind to.

Women are made to be loved, not to be understood.

Women would rather be right than reasonable.

A woman is only a woman, but a good cigar is a smoke.

Behind every successful man stands a woman – nagging, nagging, nagging.

Behind every successful man stands a woman – surprised as hell.

Behind every unsuccessful man stands a woman – saying I told you so – and the mother agrees.

*"If you thought I was great at the wedding,
wait 'til we get to the honeymoon!"*

Sometimes I wake up Grumpy. Other times I let him sleep.

A good wife and health – are a man's best wealth.

A toast to the groom – and discretion to his bachelor friends.

Down the hatch, to a striking match!

It's been said that marriage is a device of society designed to make trouble between two people who would otherwise get along very well.

A woman worries about the future until she gets a husband. A man never worries about the future until he gets a wife.

Husbands seldom realize that when they say "I do" ... they do everything.

A woman marries a man expecting he will change, but he doesn't. A man marries a woman expecting that she won't change ... and she does.

Men wake up as good-looking as they went to bed. Women somehow deteriorate during the night.

New shoes, red wine & big diamond rings ... these are a few of my favorite things.

Any married man should forget his mistakes. There's no use in two people remembering the same thing.

Marriage is a compromise. My husband makes the money ... and I spend it.

I always "see" better with my heart.

Remember to always make the little decisions with your head and the big decisions with your heart.

May you both unite as a single soul dwelling in two bodies.

I knew I married "Mr. Wright." I just didn't realize his first name was "always."

Remember that no matter how thin you slice it, there are always two sides.

Someone once said: "Criticism never built a house, wrote a play, composed a song, painted a picture or improved a marriage."

It is often because two people are so different from each other that they have so much to share.

Every woman has two husbands – the one she is given, and the one she creates.

Once a woman decides she wants something, never underestimate her ability to get it.

I wish you both the time to celebrate the simple joys.

Forget the troubles that pass away. Give thanks for the blessings that pass your way.

May all your troubles be little ones.

Love the things you love for what they are.

The sweetest love is unconditional.

Love is nothing without friendship.

The more you love each other, the closer you will come to God.

There is nothing greater in life than to love another, and to be loved in return.

The surest way to be fully loved is to love fully.

Above all, remember this: Your love is the greatest gift you can possibly give each other.

Before marriage a man will lie awake all night thinking about something you said; after marriage, he'll fall fast asleep before you finish saying it.

If we take matrimony at its lowest, we regard it as a sort of friendship recognized by the police.

If it were not for the presents, an elopement would be preferable.

A good many things are easier said than done – including the marriage ritual.

God help the man who won't marry until he finds a perfect woman, and God help him still more if he finds her.

Marriage is an institution in which a man constantly faces the music, beginning with, "Here Comes the Bride."

A comment on the times: People do not marry as early as they used to, but they seem to marry more often.

If you want your wife to listen to what you say, just talk in your sleep.

You only get married for the second time once.

Marriage is like a dull meal with the dessert at the beginning.

First thrive and then wive.

Remember, it is as easy to marry a rich man as a poor man.

A wise woman will always let her husband have her way.

The wedding march always reminds me of the music played when soldiers go to battle.

May you both look back on the past with as much pleasure as you look forward to the future.

A good marriage is when you say, "How do I love thee, let me count the ways" – and you reach for a calculator.

Who are we kidding? A husband controls his wife like a barometer controls the weather!

You know the marriage didn't work out when the thank you notes for the presents are signed by a lawyer.

The great secret of a successful marriage is to treat all disasters as incidents and none of the incidents as disasters.

Generally the woman chooses the man who will choose her.

You think you have troubles. Two months ago my wife left me for good – and my mother-in-law didn't.

Often the difference between a successful marriage and a mediocre one consists of leaving about three or four things a day unsaid.

A sound marriage is not based on complete frankness; it is based on a sensible reticence.

The vow of fidelity is an absurd commitment, but it is the heart of marriage.

Always remember that in the grammatically correct marriage, the bride says "I do" ... and the groom says, "I will."

Remember always: Love has no endings, only beginnings.

Love is only for the young ... the middle-aged ... and the old.

A hug is worth a thousand words.

A wedding wish: May you never forget what is worth remembering, or remember what is worth forgetting.

May you *truly* live all the days of your life together.

May you never leave your marriage alive.

My opinions are my wife's, and she says I'm DAMN lucky to have them.

My wife ran off with my best friend last week. Gawd, I miss him!

My wife says if I go fishing one more time she's going to leave me. Gosh, I'm going to miss her.

Nuns have been described as women who marry God. So if they divorce Him, do they get half the universe?

Shotgun wedding: a case of wife or death.

The only one of your children who does not grow up and move away is your husband.

The theory used to be you marry an older man because they are more mature. The new theory is that men don't mature. So you might as well marry a younger one.

Bumper sticker: "No cash on premises. My wife has it all."

All marriages are happy – it's the living together afterward that causes all the problems.

May you be blessed with a wife so healthy and strong, she can pull the plow when your horse drops dead.

May you learn to perform miracles: earn a living and marry off your daughters.

Sign in a marriage counselor's window: "Out to lunch – think it over."

May the bridge you build together span a lifetime.

Don't look for the perfect spouse in each other, try to be the perfect spouse for each other.

To heck with marrying a girl who makes biscuits like her mother – I want to marry one who makes dough like her father.

I had some words with my wife, and she had some paragraphs with me.

Young Son: Is it true, Dad, I heard that in some parts of Africa a man doesn't know his wife until he marries her? Dad: That happens in most countries, son.

A happy marriage is a matter of give and take; the husband gives and the wife takes.

When a newly married man looks happy we know why. But when a man married ten years or more looks happy - we wonder why.

Married life is very frustrating. In the first year of marriage, the man speaks and the woman listens. In the second year, the woman speaks and the man listens. In the third year, they both speak and the neighbors listen.

After a quarrel, a wife said to her husband, "You know, I was a fool when I married you." And the husband replied, "Yes, dear, but I was in love and didn't notice it."

It doesn't matter how often a married man changes his job, he still ends up with the same boss.

When a man opens the door of his car for his wife, you can be sure of one thing: Either the car or wife is new.

A perfect wife is one who helps the husband with the dishes.

My wife and I were deliriously happy for 20 years. Then we met.

Are you living a life of quiet desperation – or are you married?

Marriage is a great institution – if in fact you're ready for an institution.

The big question most husbands have to decide is – are they a man or a spouse?

A husband is a person who is under the impression he bosses the house – when in reality, he only houses the boss.

Husbands are a lot like the government, they promise a lot more than they can deliver.

To speak frankly, I am not in favor of long engagements. They give people the opportunity of finding out about each other's character before marriage, which I think is never advisable.

I want to get as thin as my first husband's promises.

Marriage is when a man and woman become as one; the trouble starts when they try to decide which one.

Some people ask the secret of our long marriage. We take time to go to a restaurant two times a week. A little candlelight dinner, soft music and dancing. She goes Tuesdays, I go Fridays.

The worst reconciliation is preferable to the best divorce.

It begins with a prince kissing an angel. It ends with a baldheaded man looking across the table at a fat woman.

The average man lays down the law to his wife and then accepts all her amendments.

No married man ever pokes fun at a woman for shopping all day and buying nothing.

All men are born free, but some get married.

No woman can satisfactorily explain to herself why she married her husband.

May the garden of your life together be full and ripe and bountiful.

FAMOUS QUOTES ON MARRIAGE

Joy is not in things. It is in us. – Wagner

The time to be happy is now. The place to be happy is here. – Robert G. Ingersoll

Love is all you need. – Lennon/McCartney

Love cometh like sunshine after rain. – William Shakespeare

Love is to life what sunshine is to plants and flowers. – Tom Blandi

Love is not a matter of counting the years. It is making the years count. – William Smith

Love is what you go through together. – Thornton Wilder

Prescription for a happy marriage: Whenever you're wrong, admit it, whenever you're right, shut up. – Ogden Nash

Love must be learned, and learned again and again; there is no end to it. – Katherine Anne Porter

To love a person means to agree to grow old with them. – Albert Camus

The love we have in our youth is superficial compared to the love that an old man has for an old wife. – Will Durant

Once you have learned to love, you have learned to live. – Walter M. Germain

Love is an act of endless forgiveness, a tender look which becomes a habit. – Peter Ustinov

Never above you. Never below you. Always beside you. – Walter Winchell

Marriage is not a ceremony. It is a creation! – Charlie W. Shedd

There is no more lovely, friendly and charming relationship, communion or company than a good marriage. – Martin Luther

Sometimes the hardest thing you will have to do is endure to the end of the day. Sometimes life will be so grand that the day will seem too short. – Bernice Smith

You will truly know you are married when the bills start to come and you learn to share the toothpaste. – Bernice Smith

Remember that nothing is worth more than this day. – Goethe

Having it all doesn't necessarily mean having it all at once. – Stephanie Luethkehans

Remember that women ... and elephants ... never forget. – Dorothy Parker

I'm an excellent housekeeper. Every time I get a divorce, I keep the house. – Zsa Zsa Gabor

When a man steals your wife, there is no better revenge than to let him keep her. – Sacha Guitry

Never go to bed mad. Stay up and fight. – Phyllis Diller

Eighty percent of married men cheat in America. The rest cheat in Europe. – Jackie Mason

The great question ... which I have not been able to answer ... is, "What does a woman want?" – Freud

There's a way of transferring funds that is even faster than electronic banking. It's called marriage. – James Holt McGavran

I've been asked to say a couple of words about my husband, Fang. How about 'short' and 'cheap'? – Phyllis Diller

Marriages are made in heaven and consummated on Earth. – John Lyly

Men have a much better time of it than women; for one thing, they marry later; for another thing, they die earlier. – H.L. Mencken

The husband who wants a happy marriage should learn to keep his mouth shut and his checkbook open. – Groucho Marx

"Here's to your success!"

Background on the Author

Tom Haibeck, APR is a Vancouver marketing and communications consultant who has served as Master of Ceremonies at hundreds of weddings, special events, meetings and receptions.

He began his career in the communications industry as a radio newscaster and reporter. He later attended Simon Fraser University in Vancouver, Canada, graduating with a Bachelor of Arts degree, majoring in communications.

After university, Tom worked for several large advertising and public relations agencies before launching his own communications firm in 1988. Since that time, The Haibeck Communications Group Inc. (www.Haibeck.com) has provided strategic marketing and communications services to some of the leading companies in Canada and the United States.

Tom is past president of the British Columbia Chapter of the American Marketing Association, and is an accredited member of the Canadian Public Relations Society. He has served on numerous professional and community boards, including the National Advertising Benevolent Society, Family Services of the North Shore and Simon Fraser University's Alumni Journal Editorial Advisory Board.

Tom and his family live in North Vancouver, British Columbia.